ONE DIRECTION

By Marie Morreale

Children's Press®
An Imprint of Scholastic Inc.
New York Toronto London Auckland Sydney
Mexico City New Delhi Hong Kong
Danbury, Connecticut

MEET

One Direction takes the stage at a music festival in 2012.

Photographs ©: Corbis Images: 30 bottom, 31 bottom (Splash News), 30 top left (Turgeon/Steffman/Splash News); Dreamstime: 25 bottom (Alexandr Blinov), 25 center left (Ivan Kmit), 21 top (Ksena2009), 17 top (Msphotographic); Everett Collection: 9 bottom; Getty Images: cover (Christopher Polk), 28 top (Cindy Ord), 1, 46, 47 (Danny Martindale), 28, 29 bottom left (Dave M. Benett/WireImage), 37 (Gilbert Carrasquillo/FilmMagic), 17 bottom right (Ian Horrocks/Newcastle United), 29 bottom right (Janette Pellegrini/WireImage), 40 (Jon Furniss/WireImage), 6 background, 7, 22, 23 (Juan Naharro Gimenez), 33 top (Kevin Mazu), 34 (Mathis Wienand), 10 (Scott Legato), 21 bottom (Sean Gardner), 2, 3 (Tiziana Fabi/AFP); iStockphoto/Brendan Hunter: 42 left, 42 center, 42 right, 43 left; Newscom: 41 top (DSDD/JRAB/ZOB/ZDF WENN Photos), 26 (Guillaume Horcajuelo/EPA), 22 (infausy-10/12/17/INFphoto.com), 14 right, 14 bottom (infusny-146/Roger Wong/INFphoto.com), 6 left (Nancy Rivera/Splash News), 29 top (PacificCoastNews); Redux/Camera Press: back cover; Reuters: 39 second from top right (Andrew Kelly), 4, 5, 44 (Lucy Nicholson); REX USA : 18 left (BEImages/Jim Smeal), 18 right (BEImages/Matt Baron), 14 center (Beretta/Sims), 32 top, 33 bottom (David Fisher), 6 center, 39 third from top right (Everett Collection), 39 top right (Henry Lamb/Photowire), 39 bottom right (Matt Baron), 30 top right (Newspix/Nathan Richter), 6 right (Nils Jorgensen), 13 bottom left (Owen Sweeney), 14 left, 32 bottom; Shutterstock, Inc.: 21 center right (Africa Studio), 41 bottom (Dan Kosmayer), 25 center right (M. Unal Ozmen), 38 background (My Life Graphic), 39 background (Nonnakrit); Thinkstock: 9 center, 38 background, 39 background (conejota), 9 top (IanJTurner), 25 top (Igor Kovalchuk), 13 bottom right (Oleksii_Sagitov), 38 left (seregam), 13 center (tarasov_vl), 38 right, 39 left (WimL); Yorkshire Tea: 17 bottom left; Zuma Press: 10, 11, 19 (Duncan Nicholls), 8, 12, 14, 15, 16, 20, 24, 39 top left, 39 third from top left, 39 second from bottom left, 39 bottom left, 39 second from top left, 43 right (Laura Ashman), 31 top (Robert Duyos).

Library of Congress Cataloging-in-Publication Data
Morreale, Marie.
 One Direction / by Marie Morreale.
   pages cm. — (Real bios)
 Includes bibliographical references and index.
 ISBN 978-0-531-21196-0 (lib. bdg.) — ISBN 978-0-531-21271-4 (pbk.)
 1. One Direction (Musical group)—Juvenile literature.
 2. Rock musicians—England—Biography—Juvenile literature. I. Title.
 ML3930.O66M67 2014
 782.42164092'2—dc23 [B]   2014004441

All rights reserved. Published in 2015 by Children's Press, an imprint of Scholastic Inc.
Printed in the United States of America 113

1 2 3 4 5 6 7 8 9 10 R 24 23 22 21 20 19 18 17 16 15

ONE DIRECTION!

Harry Styles . . . **Niall Horan** . . . **Louis Tomlinson** . . . **Zayn Malik** . . . **Liam Payne**—these are the **lads** of **One Direction**. The fab five have come from England and Ireland and taken the world by storm. They have broken music records everywhere and won millions of fans, who are called Directioners. In this book, you will discover how the guys fell in love with music and became besties. You might even find out some delicious details you didn't know before. Best of all, reading this book will definitely be #FUN!

CONTENTS

The boys perform "One Thing" from an elevated stage at the 2012 MTV Video Music Awards.

ALL HAIL HARRY!

LET'S HEAR IT FOR THE BOY

When Harry Styles was born, his family knew he was special. They were right! As a boy, he loved performing for family and friends. As a tween, Harry was still a natural entertainer, but he also enjoyed sports, school, and hanging out with friends. Then, as a teen, the magic struck. Harry had pop star dreams!

HE'S SO SILLY!

"YOUR FAMILY ARE THE MOST IMPORTANT [PEOPLE] TO YOU."

Harry appears on a Spanish talk show in 2012.

"I was just like every other teenager—I was in school and I had a weekend job in a bakery, which was great," he told *American Idol* host Ryan Seacrest. "I was in a band with some friends from school. I watched *The X Factor* religiously. . . . I would always watch with my mum. . . . On the final of [the sixth season], I said to my mum, 'I want to have a go at it one day.'"

Harry's mother took action and put in an application for *The X Factor*. A few weeks later she told Harry he had an audition for the show. "I was like, 'What? . . . Cool!'" Harry recalled. "Everything happened in that moment and it's been so amazing since."

funfact:
Harry has more than **20 million** Twitter followers!

FULL NAME Harry Edward Styles

BIRTHDAY February 1, 1994

BIRTHPLACE Holmes Chapel, Cheshire, England

ASTROLOGICAL SIGN Aquarius

PARENTS Mom, Anne Cox; dad, Des Styles; stepdad, Robin Twist

SIBLING Older sister, Gemma

FIRST BAND White Eskimo

FIRST JOB Part-time at W. Mandeville Bakery in Holmes Chapel

FUN FACT 1 Harry named the band One Direction

HIDDEN HAIR When he was very young, Harry had straight hair

FAVORITE DRINK Apple juice

FAMILY FUN Harry's nicknames are Hazza and H

SILLY STUFF His band nickname is Mrs. Mop because he likes to keep the tour bus clean

FUN FACT 2 Harry plays the kazoo!

SECRET TALENT Juggling

FAVORITE COLOR Orange

BIGGEST FEAR Snakes

FAVORITE FAST FOOD Tacos

FIRST PETS Harry has a dog named Max and once had a hamster named Hamster

SUPERPOWER If Harry could choose a superpower, it would be time travel

SECOND LANGUAGE French

TWITTER NAME @Harry_Styles

FAVORITE CANDY Twix

FAVORITE BOOK Harry Potter and the Sorcerer's Stone

FAVORITE FOOD Sweet corn

LEAST FAVORITE FOOD Mayonnaise

CELEB CRUSH Jennifer Lawrence

HELLO NIALL!

HIS DREAMS ARE COMING TRUE!

One of Niall Horan's first memories involved singing. It was his first love. Niall sang at home, in the car, at school, or anywhere he could. He performed in school concerts and in the choir. But the deal was sealed when Niall played the lead in a school production of *Oliver!* By the time he was 12, Niall was singing and playing the guitar in local talent competitions.

HE LOVES HIS GUITAR!

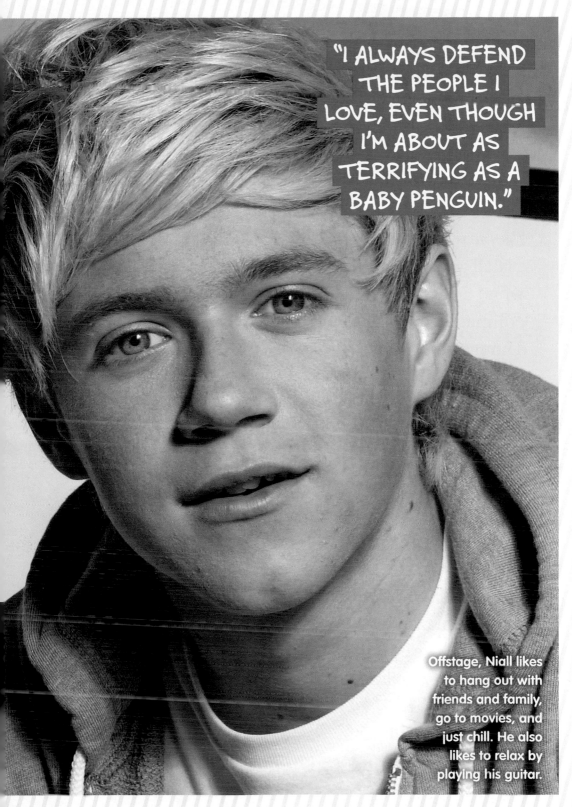

"I ALWAYS DEFEND THE PEOPLE I LOVE, EVEN THOUGH I'M ABOUT AS TERRIFYING AS A BABY PENGUIN."

Offstage, Niall likes to hang out with friends and family, go to movies, and just chill. He also likes to relax by playing his guitar.

That prepared Niall for his next step—*The X Factor*. "I'd always wanted to give *The X Factor* a go—just like anyone else in the country who enjoys singing," he told *People* magazine.

Niall got his wish when he was picked to compete on *The X Factor*. Though Niall didn't make it to the "boot camp" stage as a solo artist, guest judge Nicole Scherzinger suggested Niall, Harry, Louis, Liam, and Zayn become a group. As the boys worked together, they became One Direction. Niall is amazed by the group's success, but more importantly, he has said that because of *The X Factor* he met his four best friends.

funfact: Niall **wore braces** to straighten his teeth.

FULL NAME Niall James Horan

BIRTHDAY September 12, 1993

BIRTHPLACE Mullingar, County Westmeath, Ireland

ASTROLOGICAL SIGN Virgo

PARENTS Mom, Maura Gallagher; dad, Bobby Horan

SIBLING Older brother, Greg

MUSICAL INSTRUMENT Guitar—his favorite is a Taylor 184 series

GOOD LUCK ITEM A pair of white socks

FAVORITE SPORTS Soccer and golf

FAVORITE ROCK BAND Bon Jovi

FAVORITE SNACK Battered sausage and chips (chips are what British people call french fries)

FAVORITE RESTAURANT Nando's

FAVORITE MOVIE Grease

FAVORITE COLOR Blue

FAVORITE DRINK Water or Coca-Cola

FAVORITE VIDEO GAMES FIFA and Wii Tennis

FAVORITE SCHOOL SUBJECT Geography

FAVORITE SNEAKERS Supra

BIGGEST FEAR Pigeons. "One once flew in through my bathroom window and went for me," Niall said.

FAVORITE CLOTHES Polo shirt and cardigan sweater

SUPERPOWER If Niall could choose a superpower, it would be invisibility

BEST PRESENT His first guitar

TWITTER NAME @NiallOfficial

HOLLA! LOUIS!

HIS BIG CHOICE —SOCCER OR SINGING!

Louis Tomlinson loves to laugh! Just ask his four younger sisters—they say he was always good for a giggle. As a boy, Louis also spent a lot of time playing soccer and even had hopes of becoming a professional player. But then something else pushed those dreams aside. He realized he wanted to be an entertainer. Louis actuall

1D HAT MAN!

"I CAN'T DANCE. WHEN I DANCE, IT'S ALWAYS A JOKE!"

Louis loves writing songs. His favorite is "The Story of My Life." He wrote it with Harry, Liam, Niall, and Zayne for *Midnight Memories*.

started out as an actor and appeared in several British TV series and films. But eventually his true talent blossomed— singing.

"It was actually late that I realized it would be a dream," Louis told *People*. "I only started singing when I was 14."

Louis joined a band called The Rogue when he was in high school. However, it was a school production of *Grease* that gave him his real start. He had the lead role of Danny Zuko. "It is still one of my proudest achievements," he explained to *People*.

Of course, his next big step was *The X Factor* and becoming part of One Direction. Now, that's a goal!

funfact:
Louis named his **first** **car** Cheryl.

FULL NAME Louis William Tomlinson

BIRTHDAY December 24, 1991

BIRTHPLACE Doncaster, Yorkshire, England

ASTROLOGICAL SIGN Capricorn

PARENTS Mom, Johannah Poulston; dad, Troy Austin

SIBLINGS Charlotte "Lottie"; Felicite "Fizzy"; twins Phoebe and Daisy; twins Ernest and Doris; Georgia

INSTRUMENT Piano

FIRST AMBITION To be a drama teacher

FAVORITE DRINK Yorkshire tea

FAVORITE SNACK Cookie dough

FAVORITE FOODS Pasta and pizza

FIRST MEAL LOUIS COOKED "I made chicken breast wrapped in ham, homemade mashed potatoes, and gravy."

FAVORITE VEGETABLE Carrots

FAVORITE COLOR Red

FAVORITE SPORTS Soccer and surfing

FAVORITE FASHION ACCESSORY Suspenders

LEAST FAVORITE FOOD Baked beans

SPORTSMAN Louis plays soccer with the pro British team Doncaster Rovers

SUPERPOWER If Louis could choose a superpower, it would be to fly

FAVORITE SCHOOL PLAY Grease

TWITTER NAME @Louis_Tomlinson

CHEERIO! ZAYN!

THE SHY GUY BECOMES A STAR!

Zayn's first memory was going to a fair in his hometown of Bradford with his mother and grandmother. Zayn was very excited about this adventure. "I remember the bright lights and the thrill of going on the merry-go-round," he told *Life Story*.

Little did he know that years later, he would be on another adventure. He would be center stage with 1D, and the bright lights would be shining

HIS BLOND STREAK!

"I HAD CONFIDENCE ISSUES. THE X FACTOR HELPED ME WITH THAT."

When Zayn auditioned for *The X Factor*, he had a secret—he doesn't dance! He was still picked to be part of One Direction!

on them! But first he had to face the competition on *The X Factor*. Though Zayn was a regular performer in school musicals, he was nervous about trying out for *The X Factor*. He applied when he was 15 and 16, but didn't show up for the auditions. Things changed when he was 17. "My mom literally dragged me there," he told *Seventeen*. "I was a very introverted, quiet and reserved person. I loved singing, but I never had any major experience doing it and I didn't know what to expect."

Zayn did take the chance, and it paid off big-time. He became a member of One Direction!

FACT FILE

funfact:
He **changed the spelling** of his name from "Zain" to "Zayn."

FULL NAME Zain Javadd "Zayn" Malik

BIRTHDAY January 12, 1993

BIRTHPLACE Bradford, West Yorkshire, England

ASTROLOGICAL SIGN Capricorn

PARENTS Mom, Patricia "Tricia" Malik; dad, Yaser Malik

SIBLINGS Older sister, Doniya; younger sisters, Waliyha and Safaa

NUMBER ONE GIRL Little Mix's Perrie Edwards

FAVORITE HOME-COOKED MEAL "I love samosas filled with mincemeat. My mum makes really great ones."

FAVORITE DINNER Fried chicken or spaghetti

FAVORITE RESTAURANT Nando's

SILLY SECRET Zayn sings Beyoncé songs in the shower

FAVORITE SAYING "Vas Happenin'?"

FAVORITE SONG Michael Jackson's "Thriller"

PRE-CONCERT HABIT Brushing his teeth

FAVORITE KIND OF MOVIES Scary

FAVORITE SINGER Justin Timberlake

FAVORITE BOOK SERIES Harry Potter

SUPERPOWER If Zayn could choose a superpower, it would be to fly

FIRST AMBITION To be a science teacher

BIGGEST FEARS Heights and the dark

FIRST JOB A waiter at a family restaurant

BAD HABIT Biting his lower lip

HOBBY Drawing **caricatures**

TWITTER NAME @zaynmalik

WHAT'S UP? LIAM!

EVERY DAY IS AMAZING FOR HIM!

was born three weeks early, and I kept being ill," Liam told *People*. "I was always in [the] hospital having tests done, but they couldn't find out what was wrong."

Finally, doctors discovered that one of Liam's kidneys wasn't working properly. Liam had to be careful and live a very healthy lifestyle, but his illness didn't stop him from taking boxing lessons and joining his school's cross-country running

HE LOVES TO SURF!

"I HAVE THE BEST DANCE MOVES. I'M KING OF THE DANCE FLOOR!"

In February 2014, Liam had a dream come true: He passed his driving test. You better believe he was happy, happy, happy!

team. Sports were a major part of his life, but music was number one. He loved singing and was always up for a **karaoke** night. When Liam was 14, his dad, Geoff, urged him to try out for *The X Factor*. He was dropped after reaching the final group of 24 contestants. Instead of quitting, Liam took vocal lessons and performed wherever he could get a **gig**. At 17, Liam auditioned for *The X Factor* again. This time, he found the right direction—One Direction.

On top of his fab-five success, Liam got another bit of good news—his kidney problem cleared up when he was 19. No wonder Liam is happy every day!

FACT FILE

funfact: Liam's **band nickname** is Daddy Direction.

FULL NAME Liam James Payne

BIRTHDAY August 29, 1993

BIRTHPLACE Wolverhamptom, West Midlands, England

ASTROLOGICAL SIGN Virgo

PARENTS Mom, Karen Payne; and dad, Geoff Payne

SIBLINGS Older sisters, Ruth and Nicola

INSTRUMENTS Piano and guitar

FAVORITE ANIMAL Turtles

HOBBY Drawing

SUPER WISH To sing on the moon

FAVORITE HIGH SCHOOL SPORT Track

FAVORITE SANDWICH Ham

FAVORITE FAST FOOD Chicken fingers

FAVORITE MOVIES The Toy Story series

FAVORITE CANDY Chocolate

BIGGEST FEAR Spoons

FAVORITE BOARD GAME Monopoly

FAVORITE COLOR Purple

FAVORITE SPORTS Soccer, basketball, and boxing

FAVORITE LAPTOP MacBook Pro

FAVORITE DRINK Coca-Cola

WORST HABIT He's a worrier

SUPERPOWER If Liam could choose a superpower, it would be invisibility

SILLY STUFF Liam can talk like Kermit the Frog

SECRET DREAMS Liam wishes he could take a trip to outer space

TWITTER NAME @Real_Liam_Payne

The boys arrive on the red carpet at a French awards show in 2013.

HOW THEY BECAME THE NEXT BIG THING!

FROM *THE X FACTOR* TO NUMBER ONE IN THE WORLD

When *The X Factor* judge Simon Cowell decided to create the group One Direction from solo acts Harry Styles, Niall Horan, Louis Tomlinson, Zayn Malik, and Liam Payne, the boys were thrilled to have a second chance in the competition. They didn't win the seventh season of *The X Factor*—they came in third place. But that didn't matter. Within a year, the lads from England and Ireland became one of the most successful bands in the world! Their fans, called Directioners, numbered in the millions and came from every continent.

Because of Twitter, Facebook, and other social media, they were popular in the United States even before they appeared on stage. In February 2012, when they released their first single, "What Makes You Beautiful," the fandemonium was loud and clear. 1D performed their first American concert as the opening act for Nickelodeon's TV and music stars Big Time Rush at Chicago's Rosemont Theater. The sold-out audience—4,400 strong—amazed 1D by actually knowing the lyrics to their songs! It was clear that a superstar band was born. That fact was confirmed when, on March 12, 2012, 1D made their first appearance on *The Today Show*. It was the day before their first album, *Up All Night*, was released in the United States, and more than 10,000 fans showed up to see them perform on the morning show.

1D continued with Big Time Rush's Better

TONS OF FAN NOTES!

Directioners leave their messages at the 1D exhibit at NYC's Madame Tussauds™ wax museum.

1D'S TOP DAYS!

JULY 23, 2010
Harry, Niall, Louis, Zayn, and Liam come together to form One Direction on *The X Factor*.

OCTOBER 2, 2010
1D sings their first song on the seventh season of *The X Factor*.

1D poses with Simon Cowell.

DECEMBER 11, 2010
1D wins third place on *The X Factor*.

◆ 1D thrills a crowd at the Picture House in Edinburgh, Scotland.

With U tour and then **headlined** their own Up All Night tour in the United States from May 2012 to July 2012. In November 2012, their second album, *Take Me Home*, was released. Both of their albums hit the number one spot on the *Billboard* charts, an achievement that no other boy band had ever accomplished!

The boys recorded *Take Me Home* in one month. They worked on it during a break from their tour and while they were on the road. On *Take Me Home*, all five

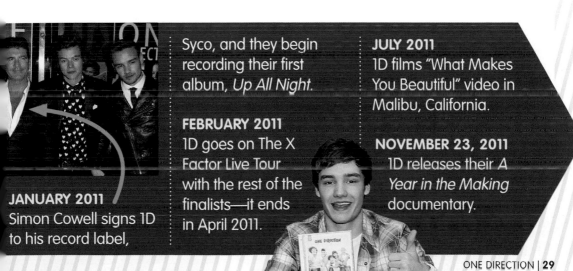

JANUARY 2011
Simon Cowell signs 1D to his record label,

Syco, and they begin recording their first album, *Up All Night*.

FEBRUARY 2011
1D goes on The X Factor Live Tour with the rest of the finalists—it ends in April 2011.

JULY 2011
1D films "What Makes You Beautiful" video in Malibu, California.

NOVEMBER 23, 2011
1D releases their *A Year in the Making* documentary.

SO HUGGABLE!

members cowrote three songs together—"Last First Kiss," "Back for You," and "Summer Love."

Zayn told *Billboard*, "Somebody could have the first initial idea after we heard a melody or a track, and someone would chip in a few words and then Liam or someone else could come in and by the end of the day we'd have a song. We wanted to feel like we were giving

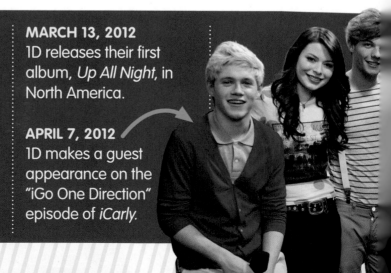

FEBRUARY 14, 2012
1D's first single, "What Makes You Beautiful," is released in the United States.

FEBRUARY 26, 2012
1D joins the Big Time Rush Better With U concert tour.

MARCH 13, 2012
1D releases their first album, *Up All Night*, in North America.

APRIL 7, 2012
1D makes a guest appearance on the "iGo One Direction" episode of *iCarly*.

a little more back in our personal lives, so what better way than to get involved in the writing process?"

In 2012, 1D racked up major credits—they appeared on Pepsi TV commercials, released the second version of their Hasbro dolls, and performed at the closing ceremonies of the 2012 Summer Olympic Games. They were also named Best Artist of the Year by MTV and Top New Artist by *Billboard*. They won trophies at the MTV Video Music Awards, the Teen Choice Awards, and the Nickelodeon Kids' Choice Awards. They closed the year with two sold-out shows at the legendary Madison Square Garden in New York City.

Fans go wild at a 1D show in Florida.

One Direction really got busy in 2013! They

MAY 22, 2012
1D's Up All Night tour starts in North America.

AUGUST 12, 2012
1D performs at the closing ceremony of

the Summer Olympics in London.

SEPTEMBER 6, 2012
1D performs at the MTV Video Music Awards.

NOVEMBER 13, 2012
1D releases their second album, *Take Me Home*.

signed a three-year/three-album deal with Sony Records in the United States, so you don't have to worry about them breaking up! Next, they started their Take Me Home world tour in Europe on February 23, then continued to North America, Australia, and New Zealand before ending in Japan on November 3. During a short summer break, they released the docu-concert movie *One Direction: This Is Us* on August 29 in London and August 30 in Los Angeles. One Direction added to their fans' summer fun by releasing the first single, "Best Song Ever," from their third studio album, *Midnight Memories*. The full album was released

LIAM TAKES A SELFIE!

DECEMBER 3, 2012
1D headlines their first appearance at New York City's Madison Square Garden.

DECEMBER 14, 2012
1D is named Top New Artist by *Billboard* magazine.

JANUARY 9, 2013
1D signs a three-year/three-album deal with Sony Records.

JUNE 13, 2013
1D starts their Take Me Home tour in North America.

AUGUST 30, 2013
1D releases their 3-D docu-concert film, *One Direction: This Is Us*, in the United States.

1D arrives at the 2013 Teen Choice Awards.

on November 25. It charted number one the first week out. The group also announced the 2014 Where We Are stadium tour. They have listed dates for South America, Europe, and North America. A whirlwind schedule! But don't worry, Harry, Niall, Louis, Zayn, and Liam love every minute of it!

NOVEMBER, 23, 2013
The "1D Day" global seven-hour live stream is broadcast.

NOVEMBER 25, 2013
1D releases their third album,

Midnight Memories, in the United States.

DECEMBER 7, 2013
1D makes their first appearance on *Saturday Night Live*.

FEBRUARY 19, 2014
1D wins the Global Success Award at the BRIT Awards.

AUGUST 1, 2014
1D starts the North American leg of their Where We Are tour.

"WE'RE JUST FIVE NORMAL BOYS FROM THE U.K."
—HARRY

One Direction's fans are very important to them. The boys know that they owe everything to their loyal Directioners.

LAUGH WITH THE LADS!

WHEN ONE DIRECTION SPEAKS, EVERYONE LISTENS!

P art of the job of being the world's number one pop group is doing interviews . . . lots of interviews! Harry, Niall, Louis, Zayn, and Liam learned that early on in their career. From the day they became One Direction on *The X Factor*, they faced reporters holding microphones and asking questions.

Everyone wanted to know every detail of the boys' lives. Magazine reporters, radio DJs, and TV journalists are just the tip of the Q & A iceberg. Fans post thousands of queries on Twitter, Facebook, Tumblr, and other social media sites. After awhile, being asked the same questions over and over became a bit dull. So, to liven things up, Harry, Niall, Louis, Zayn, and Liam chose to have fun with the questions. Reporters got used to the boys joking around during their press sessions. A 1D interview soon became a laughathon! Niall summed up the 1D approach to interviews when he spoke with British *GQ* magazine.

"We're pretty honest," he said. "We're just five guys having the time of our lives."

ZAYN

On how he wants 1D to be remembered . . . "I want a monument put up in [his hometown] Bradford! They will build statues of us."

On the hardest part of being on tour so much . . . "Being away from home so much and missing our friends and family. But then again I get to travel with four of my closest friends all around the world, so we keep ourselves positive. And fans helps us a lot as well!"

NIALL

On his biggest LOL moment . . . "I've danced with my cat before. You know when you pick up an animal and dance with it? I've done that! My cat's name is Jess, and I've had him for more than ten years."

On what he was like in high school . . . "I was very talkative—I was a people person. I was always singing . . . even now, I'll just get up and sing."

LIAM

On the silliest news story about him . . . "I lost a shoe in Paris and that made world news!"

On why 1D is not known for their dance moves . . . "We

just kind of came out and said, 'We can't dance. We're a bit lazy. We're just normal lads.'"

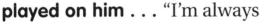

1D performs on NBC's *Today* in 2013.

HARRY

On the "walrus" prank Louis played on him . . . "I'm always falling asleep when we're on tour and wake up to find straws shoved up my nose."

On what superhero he would like to be . . . "Superman. Then actually, no I wouldn't. If you were best **mates** with Superman, you'd always be Superman's best mate."

LOUIS

On what surprised him the most when 1D opened for Big Time Rush in 2012 . . . "The fans were chanting our names. They knew the words to the songs off the album that wasn't even out in America. . . . It was amazing."

On what he likes best in a girlfriend . . . "Someone who is loyal and has a sense of humor, and is kindhearted too. Oh, and if they're tidy—that would be good because I'm not. . . . I like someone who likes a laugh."

FABULOUS TIDBITS ABOUT

HARRY, ZAYN,

FAVORITE TOUR FOOD

LIAM
Bacon, steak, and vegetables

NIALL
Sausage and mash, pies, creamy chicken pasta, or chicken Kiev

ZAYN
Pasta Bolognese or spicy chicken

LOUIS
Eats anything—but a bowl of Special K cereal is his favorite

NIALL, LOUIS, AND LIAM! CHECK THEM OUT!

ACTOR WHO SHOULD PLAY YOU IN A MOVIE

HARRY

"George Clooney [or] Orlando Bloom . . . because he [Bloom] has curly hair."

LIAM

"Jay Z."

NIALL

"Jay Z? [laughs] I . . . always say Tom Felton, who played Draco Malfoy in the Harry Potter films."

LOUIS

"I [haven't] got a clue who would play me."

ZAYN

"Robert Downey Jr."

Niall and Liam get in the Christmas spirit.

FAVORITE CHRISTMAS TRADITIONS

NIALL

"[I] go home to Ireland and do the same thing as every year: drink, eat, and sleep a lot. Just chill out, become fat."

HARRY

"Christmas dinner. You go in hard. Then about 7 o'clock, watching a film, you make a turkey sandwich."

LOUIS

"My nana cooks us a classic dinner of chicken, stuffing, roasted potatoes, and loads of gravy."

FAVE CLOTHES

LOUIS
A striped top

ZAYN
Red varsity jacket

LIAM
Plain white tee

HARRY
A new tan trench coat

NIALL
Supra sneakers

FAVORITE ICE CREAM

LIAM
Double chocolate brownie

LOUIS
Yorkshire Tea—a British tea maker made it especially for Louis!

ZAYN
Strawberry cheesecake

HARRY & NIALL
Honeycomb

FAVORITE SUPERHEROES

LIAM & LOUIS
Iron Man

NIALL & ZAYN
The Hulk

HARRY
Superman

TELLING TALES ON EACH OTHER

ZAYN ON LOUIS

"Louis makes all of us lads laugh all the time. He is just the life and soul of the party!"

LIAM ON NIALL

"Niall — he exaggerates everything — good and bad!"

HARRY ON ZAYN

"Zayn is quiet, but very funny, and quite strange."

LIAM ON HARRY

"They are all flirts, but [Harry] is the king of flirts. Harry is the cheeky little chappy."

LOUIS ON LIAM

"Liam is quite sensible. . . . He kind of brings us down a level if we're being too mischievous."

1D accepts the award for Best New Artist at the 2012 MTV Video Music Awards.

WHAT THE FUTURE HOLDS

WILL THEY BE THE ALL-TIME #1 BAND?

What more can One Direction do? They've won major music awards, sold out every concert, and are followed by millions of die-hard "Directioners." They've traveled all over the world, had every one of their albums—*Up All Night, Take Me Home*, and *Midnight Memories*—reach the number one spot on music charts, filmed a top box office film, published books, created fragrance and nail polish lines, and earned the number one spot on the richest British stars under 30 list in 2013 (their total earnings were $963,960,000). One Direction strained

Web sites every time they made an announcement or hosted an Internet event. One Direction had a first-ever worldwide event on November 23, 2013—"1D Day." On that Saturday, fans all over the world were able to watch and interact with a seven-hour 1D live stream.

Believe it or not, for Harry, Niall, Louis, Zayn, and Liam, this is just the beginning. They have signed contracts lasting to 2016 with both their British and American record labels, so fans can expect more albums. The band's 2014 Where We Are stadium world tour has added concert dates as it rolls out. Reportedly, they have a high-tech recording studio traveling with them on tour so they can work on their fourth album, to be released in 2014. And mentor Simon Cowell teased MTV News that there might be a second film in the works. "Yeah, for sure, we'd love to do another movie with them," he said.

And that's just a few predictions for One Direction. The fivesome definitely has a lot more fun to share!

> "A FEW MONTHS AGO WE DECIDED TO GIVE BACK SOMETHING TO ALL THE FANS THAT HAVE SUPPORTED US." —HARRY

> "WE'VE HAD SUCH AN AMAZING THREE YEARS AND WE COULDN'T HAVE DONE IT WITHOUT YOU GUYS. SO WE PUT ALL OUR HEADS TOGETHER AND CAME UP WITH THE IDEA OF 1D DAY." —LOUIS

Resources

BOOKS

Brooks, Riley. *One Direction: Superstardom!* New York: Scholastic, 2013.

Brooks, Riley. *One Direction Quiz Book.* New York: Scholastic, 2012.

James, Sarah-Louise. *One Direction: The Ultimate Fan Book.* Hauppauge, NY: Barron's Educational Series, Inc., 2013.

One Direction. *One Direction: Dare to Dream: Life as One Direction.* New York: HarperCollins, 2012.

One Direction. *One Direction: Where We Are.* New York: HarperCollins, 2013.

Facts for Now

Visit this Scholastic Web site for more information on **One Direction**: www.factsfornow.scholastic.com Enter the keywords **One Direction**

Glossary

caricatures *(KAR-i-kuh-choorz)* exaggerated drawings or verbal descriptions of people

gig *(GIG)* live concert

headlined *(HED-lyned)* performed as the main act at a concert

karaoke *(kar-ee-OH-kee)* a form of entertainment that originated in Japan in which people sing the words of popular songs to recorded background music

lads *(LADZ)* British slang for "boys"

mates *(MAYTS)* British slang for "friends"

Niall, Zayn, Liam, Louis, and Harry are the kings of LOL!

Index

Acknowledgments

Page 7: *Harry Blurb:* US Collector's Edition: Hot Guys! October 2013
Page 11: *Niall Blurb:* BDM's Souvenir Series: Take Me Home
Page 13: *Niall's Biggest Fear:* The Sun newspaper/pressparty.com
Page 15: *Louis Blurb:* Bop
Page 17: *First Meal Louis Cooked:* Seventeen.com, October 11, 2013
Page 19: *Zayn Blurb:* People, One Direction Collector's Special, June 2012
Page 21: *Zayn's Favorite Home-Cooked Meal:* NOW online, July 20, 2012
Page 23: *Liam Blurb:* Bop, November 2012
Page 25: *Liam Class Clown:* People, One Direction, June 2012

Page 30: *Zayn:* Billboard, December 22, 2012
Page 34: *Harry Blurb:* digitalspy.com
Page 36: *Intro—Niall Quote:* British GQ, September 2013
Page 36: *How Zayn Wants to Be Remembered:* British Glamour, September 2013
Page 36: *Zayn—Hardest Part of Touring:* Tumblr.com, July 12, 2012
Page 36: *Niall—Dancing with His Cat:* Bop, November 2012
Page 36: *Niall—in high school:* Seventeen, October 2012
Page 36: *Liam's Silliest Story:* Parade, November 18, 2012
Page 37: *Liam—Why 1D Doesn't Dance:* British Glamour, September 2013

Page 37: *Harry—Walrus Prank:* sugarscape.com, August 8, 2011
Page 37: *Harry—Favorite Superhero:* MTV News, August 27, 2013
Page 37: *Louis—Opening for Big Time Rush:* Billboard, December 14, 2012
Page 37: *Louis—Girlfriend:* Teen Now, February 1, 2011
Page 38: *Favorite Tour Food—Liam, Niall, Zayn and, Louis:* Sarah Nicholas, 1D's official tour chef—The Daily Star and MTV News
Page 39: *Actor Who Should Play Them:* Teen Now, November 2013
Page 40: *Christmas Traditions: Niall and Harry:* Parade, November 18, 2012; *Louis*: GL December 2011/January 2012

Page 41: *Fave Clothes:* Teen Vogue, May 2012
Page 41: *Favorite Ice Cream:* Teen Vogue, May 2012
Page 42: *Favorite Superheroes:* MTV News, August 2013
Page 43: *Telling Tales: Zayn on Louis*—Bop, May 2012; *Liam on Niall*—Seventeen, October 2012; *Harry on Zayn*—Scholastic Classroom Magazines, January 25, 2012; *Liam on Harry*—Triumph Books: One Direction: What Makes You Beautiful; *Louis on Liam:* People, One Direction Special, June 2012
Page 45: *1D Day: Harry and Louis*—Official 1D YouTube Channel/heatworld.com, October 3, 2012

About the Author

Marie Morreale is the author of many official and unofficial celebrity biographies. She attended New York University as an English/creative writing major and began her writing and editorial career in New York City. As the editor of teen/music magazines *Teen Machine* and *Jam!*, she covered TV, film, and music personalities and interviewed superstars such as Michael Jackson, Britney Spears, and Justin Timberlake/*NSYNC. Morreale was also an editor/writer at Little Golden Books.

Today, she is the executive editor, Media, of Scholastic Classroom Magazines writing about pop-culture, sports, news, and special events. Morreale lives in New York City and is entertained daily by her two Maine coon cats, Cher and Sullivan.